PRINCEWILL LAGANG

Success Stories of 21st Century Entrepreneurs

Contents

1

"Success Stories of 21st Century Entrepreneurs"

In the early years of the 21st century, the world witnessed a remarkable wave of entrepreneurial success stories that changed the way we think about business and innovation. These stories serve as a source of inspiration for aspiring entrepreneurs and a testament to the endless possibilities of the modern business landscape. In this chapter, we will explore a few of these extraordinary success stories, highlighting the challenges these entrepreneurs faced, the innovative ideas that drove their success, and the lasting impact they've had on our world.

1.1: The Rise of Silicon Valley

Our journey begins in the heart of the tech world, Silicon Valley, where the 21st century saw the rise of several iconic entrepreneurs. One of the most notable is Mark Zuckerberg, the co-founder of Facebook. We'll delve into his story, from the Harvard dorm room where he conceived the idea to the global social media giant that connects over 2.8 billion people today.

1.2: The E-Commerce Revolution

Moving beyond the world of social media, we'll explore the rise of e-commerce giants like Jeff Bezos, the visionary founder of Amazon. We'll trace the growth of this online marketplace from its humble beginnings as an online bookseller to its current status as one of the world's largest e-commerce and cloud computing companies.

1.3: The Sharing Economy and Uber

The sharing economy emerged as a disruptive force in the 21st century, led by companies like Uber. We'll delve into the story of Travis Kalanick and Garrett Camp, the founders of Uber, and how they revolutionized the transportation industry with a simple smartphone app.

1.4: Sustainable Innovation and Tesla

Elon Musk, one of the most iconic entrepreneurs of the 21st century, has made significant strides in sustainable technology and space exploration through his companies, including Tesla. We'll explore Musk's journey from co-founding PayPal to leading the electric car revolution and the quest for sustainable energy solutions.

1.5: Health-Tech and Theranos

Not all success stories are without controversy, as we'll see in the case of Elizabeth Holmes and her company, Theranos. We'll examine the rise and fall of this health-tech startup and the lessons to be learned from its story.

1.6: The Unconventional Path of Richard Branson

Richard Branson, the founder of the Virgin Group, followed an unconventional path to success by taking risks in various industries, from music to airlines and space exploration. We'll explore his unique entrepreneurial journey and the lessons it offers.

1.7: Female Entrepreneurs: The Case of Sarah Blakely

Diving into the world of female entrepreneurship, we'll spotlight Sarah Blakely, the founder of Spanx. Her story demonstrates how innovation, determination, and a willingness to disrupt traditional industries can lead to remarkable success.

1.8: The New Wave of Social Impact Entrepreneurs

The 21st century also saw the emergence of entrepreneurs driven by a desire to make a positive impact on society. We'll discuss the stories of individuals like Blake Mycoskie, the founder of TOMS, and his pioneering "One for One" business model.

1.9: The Global Reach of Alibaba

Jack Ma, the founder of Alibaba, changed the landscape of e-commerce not only in China but around the world. We'll explore Ma's entrepreneurial journey and the international impact of his company.

1.10: From Entrepreneur to Philanthropist: Bill Gates

Concluding our exploration of 21st-century success stories, we'll take a look at Bill Gates, who transitioned from co-founding Microsoft to becoming a leading philanthropist. His journey reflects the potential for entrepreneurs to leverage their success for global benefit.

Throughout this chapter, we'll not only recount the achievements of these entrepreneurs but also uncover the principles and qualities that contributed to their remarkable success. Their stories serve as a testament to the entrepreneurial spirit of the 21st century and inspire future generations to dream big, take risks, and make a lasting impact on the world through innovation and determination.

2

"Navigating the Entrepreneurial Landscape"

In the fast-paced world of entrepreneurship in the 21st century, success is not guaranteed, and the road to achieving one's goals is often filled with challenges, uncertainties, and opportunities. In this chapter, we will explore the essential principles and strategies that aspiring entrepreneurs can use to navigate the complex entrepreneurial landscape. We will delve into the key aspects of starting and sustaining a business in today's competitive environment.

2.1: Identifying Opportunities

Successful entrepreneurs are often those who have a keen eye for identifying opportunities. We'll discuss how to recognize market gaps, emerging trends, and unmet needs, and we'll look at case studies of entrepreneurs who turned innovative ideas into thriving businesses.

2.2: The Business Plan

Every journey begins with a plan. We'll explore the importance of a well-crafted business plan and how it serves as a roadmap for entrepreneurs, helping them define their vision, set goals, and secure funding.

2.3: Building the Right Team

Behind every successful entrepreneur is a dedicated and skilled team. We'll discuss the art of assembling the right people with complementary skills and the culture that fosters innovation, creativity, and resilience.

2.4: Funding Your Venture

Access to capital is often a significant hurdle for entrepreneurs. We'll explore various sources of funding, including venture capital, angel investors, crowdfunding, and bootstrapping, and the pros and cons of each.

2.5: Risk Management

Entrepreneurship involves taking risks, but successful entrepreneurs are not reckless. We'll examine how to assess, mitigate, and manage risks effectively to ensure the sustainability of a business.

2.6: Marketing and Branding

In the age of digital marketing, we'll delve into the strategies and techniques that entrepreneurs use to build and promote their brands. We'll also explore the importance of understanding your target audience and crafting compelling marketing messages.

2.7: Adapting to Change

The business world is ever-evolving, and adaptability is a key trait of successful entrepreneurs. We'll discuss how to embrace change, pivot when necessary, and stay ahead of the curve.

2.8: Ethics and Social Responsibility

In an era where social responsibility is increasingly important, we'll explore how entrepreneurs can balance profit with ethical considerations and contribute positively to society.

2.9: Technology and Innovation

The role of technology in modern entrepreneurship cannot be overstated. We'll discuss how staying up-to-date with technological advancements and fostering a culture of innovation can set entrepreneurs apart.

2.10: Lessons from Failure

Not all entrepreneurial journeys end in success. We'll examine the lessons that can be learned from failure and how resilience and the ability to bounce back are critical traits for aspiring entrepreneurs.

2.11: Scaling and Growth

Scaling a business from a small startup to a global enterprise is a significant challenge. We'll explore the strategies and tactics that entrepreneurs use to manage growth and expansion effectively.

2.12: The Role of Networking

Building and maintaining a network of contacts can open doors and provide valuable insights. We'll discuss the importance of networking and how it can help entrepreneurs advance their ventures.

Throughout this chapter, we will draw from the experiences of successful entrepreneurs, sharing their insights and strategies for navigating the entrepreneurial landscape. By understanding and applying these principles, aspiring entrepreneurs can increase their chances of success, adapt to the ever-changing business world, and make a meaningful impact on their industries and society.

3

"Innovation and Disruption: The Engine of Entrepreneurship"

In the 21st century, innovation and disruption have become the driving forces behind the success of many entrepreneurs and their ventures. This chapter explores the critical role of innovation in entrepreneurship, showcasing how entrepreneurs identify opportunities, create groundbreaking solutions, and disrupt traditional industries to usher in a new era of business.

3.1: The Innovation Mindset

We begin by delving into the innovation mindset and the characteristics that set innovative entrepreneurs apart. We'll explore attributes like creativity, problem-solving, adaptability, and the willingness to challenge the status quo.

3.2: The Power of Creativity

Creativity is at the heart of entrepreneurship. We'll examine how entrepreneurs harness their creativity to generate new ideas, products, and services. Case studies will highlight how creative thinking leads to break-throughs.

3.3: Market Disruption

Disruptive innovation is a term often associated with modern entrepreneurship. We'll explore how entrepreneurs identify industries ripe for disruption and the strategies they use to challenge existing market leaders.

3.4: Innovation and Technology

The relationship between entrepreneurship and technology is inseparable. We'll discuss how technological advancements have enabled entrepreneurs to develop new products and services, enter new markets, and redefine entire industries.

3.5: The Role of Research and Development

Successful entrepreneurs invest in research and development (R&D) to drive innovation. We'll explore how R&D plays a pivotal role in the development of cutting-edge solutions and products.

3.6: Open Innovation

Innovation is not limited to internal efforts. We'll discuss how entrepreneurs leverage open innovation, collaborating with external partners, customers, and even competitors to foster fresh ideas and develop revolutionary solutions.

3.7: Intellectual Property and Innovation

Protecting intellectual property is a significant concern for innovative entrepreneurs. We'll delve into the importance of patents, trademarks, and copyrights in safeguarding innovative ideas.

3.8: Sustainable Innovation

The 21st century has witnessed a growing emphasis on sustainable and socially responsible innovation. We'll explore how entrepreneurs are developing eco-friendly and socially conscious solutions.

3.9: Innovation Across Industries

Innovation isn't exclusive to the tech sector. We'll examine how entrepreneurs in various industries, from healthcare to agriculture, have introduced groundbreaking ideas and technologies.

3.10: The Startup Ecosystem

Innovation thrives in supportive ecosystems. We'll look at how various players, including incubators, accelerators, and venture capitalists, contribute to the entrepreneurial ecosystem.

3.11: Innovation Challenges and Risks

Innovation is not without its challenges and risks. We'll discuss the potential obstacles entrepreneurs face when introducing new concepts and products and how they navigate these hurdles.

3.12: Case Studies of Innovative Entrepreneurs

Throughout this chapter, we'll showcase case studies of pioneering entrepreneurs like Elon Musk, Elon Musk, Steve Jobs, and others, highlighting their groundbreaking innovations and the impact they've had on their respective industries and the world.

By the end of this chapter, readers will have a deep understanding of the pivotal role of innovation in modern entrepreneurship. They will also gain insights into how innovative thinking and disruptive solutions can lead to entrepreneurial success and transform the way we live and do business.

4

"The Entrepreneurial Ecosystem: Nurturing Success"

Behind every successful entrepreneur, there is an ecosystem of support, resources, and networks that plays a crucial role in nurturing their ventures. In this chapter, we will explore the various components of the entrepreneurial ecosystem and how they contribute to the success and growth of entrepreneurs and their businesses in the 21st century.

4.1: The Elements of the Ecosystem

We start by dissecting the different elements of the entrepreneurial ecosystem, which include government policies, educational institutions, mentorship programs, and more. Understanding these components is essential for aspiring entrepreneurs looking to leverage the ecosystem to their advantage.

4.2: Government Support and Policies

Government policies and initiatives can have a significant impact on entrepreneurship. We'll explore how governments worldwide are fostering entrepreneurial environments through incentives, funding, and regulatory changes.

4.3: The Role of Educational Institutions

Universities and educational institutions are not only centers of learning but also hubs for innovation and entrepreneurship. We'll discuss how academic institutions are nurturing the next generation of entrepreneurs through courses, incubators, and research programs.

4.4: Incubators and Accelerators

Incubators and accelerators provide startups with the resources, mentorship, and networking opportunities they need to grow rapidly. We'll examine how these programs work and their benefits for entrepreneurs.

4.5: The Investment Landscape

Access to capital is vital for entrepreneurial success. We'll delve into the various forms of investment, from angel investors to venture capital, and how entrepreneurs secure funding for their ventures.

4.6: Networking and Mentorship

Networking and mentorship play a critical role in an entrepreneur's journey. We'll explore how connecting with experienced mentors and building a strong professional network can open doors and provide guidance.

4.7: Innovation Hubs and Clusters

Certain regions and cities have become known for their vibrant entrepreneurial communities. We'll highlight the concept of innovation hubs and clusters, exploring how they foster collaboration and innovation.

4.8: Access to Resources

Entrepreneurs need access to resources such as co-working spaces, legal services, and marketing support. We'll discuss how these resources contribute to the success of startups.

4.9: Diversity and Inclusion

The entrepreneurial ecosystem is increasingly emphasizing diversity and inclusion. We'll examine the importance of promoting underrepresented entrepreneurs and how it benefits the ecosystem as a whole.

4.10: Measuring Success and Impact

Quantifying the impact of the entrepreneurial ecosystem is a complex task. We'll explore the various metrics and methods used to measure the success and effectiveness of ecosystem support.

4.11: Global Perspectives on Ecosystems

We'll take a global perspective, looking at how different countries and regions have developed unique entrepreneurial ecosystems and how these ecosystems have influenced their economic growth.

4.12: Challenges and the Future of Ecosystems

The entrepreneurial ecosystem is not without challenges. We'll discuss the potential hurdles and the future outlook for entrepreneurial support systems in an ever-changing world.

Throughout this chapter, readers will gain a comprehensive understanding of how the entrepreneurial ecosystem provides essential support for startups and entrepreneurs. Whether you're a budding entrepreneur or an ecosystem builder, this chapter will offer insights into the dynamic and interconnected elements that contribute to entrepreneurial success in the 21st century.

5

"The Art of Leadership in Entrepreneurship"

Effective leadership is a cornerstone of successful entrepreneurship in the 21st century. In this chapter, we explore the critical role of leadership in guiding businesses to success, fostering innovation, and navigating the challenges of the modern entrepreneurial landscape.

5.1: The Entrepreneurial Leader's Profile

We start by examining the characteristics and qualities that define a successful entrepreneurial leader. From vision and resilience to adaptability and a growth mindset, we delve into what it takes to lead effectively.

5.2: Leading by Example

Effective leaders often lead by example, setting the tone for their organizations. We explore how entrepreneurs inspire their teams through their actions, values, and commitment to the mission.

5.3: The Visionary Leader

Vision is a driving force in entrepreneurship. We discuss how visionary leaders develop and communicate a clear and compelling vision that motivates their teams and inspires innovation.

5.4: Building and Managing Teams

Entrepreneurial leaders must be adept at assembling and managing diverse teams. We explore the art of team building, fostering collaboration, and aligning team members with the organization's goals.

5.5: Leading Through Change

The entrepreneurial landscape is marked by rapid change. We discuss how effective leaders lead their organizations through uncertainty and transformation, helping them adapt and thrive.

5.6: Decision-Making and Risk Management

Leaders make critical decisions that impact the direction and success of their ventures. We delve into the decision-making process, risk assessment, and the art of making informed choices in the face of uncertainty.

5.7: Communication Skills

Effective communication is paramount for leaders. We explore how entrepreneurs convey their vision, build strong relationships, and navigate challenging conversations with stakeholders.

5.8: Ethical Leadership

In an era of increased scrutiny on business ethics, we discuss the importance of ethical leadership and how it influences an organization's reputation and long-term success.

5.9: Resilience and Adaptability

Entrepreneurial leaders face setbacks and obstacles. We examine how resilience and adaptability are essential qualities for navigating the highs and lows of entrepreneurship.

5.10: Leadership Styles

There are various leadership styles, each with its strengths and weaknesses. We discuss different leadership approaches, such as transformational, servant, and situational leadership, and when to employ them.

5.11: Mentoring and Coaching

Mentoring and coaching play a crucial role in developing the next generation of leaders. We explore how entrepreneurial leaders can mentor others and the benefits of this practice.

5.12: The Legacy of Entrepreneurial Leadership

We conclude by examining the lasting impact of entrepreneurial leaders like Steve Jobs, Elon Musk, and others, and how their leadership styles have shaped the companies they founded and the industries they disrupted.

By the end of this chapter, readers will have a comprehensive understanding of the multifaceted role of leadership in entrepreneurship. Whether you're an aspiring entrepreneur, a business leader, or someone interested in understanding the dynamics of leadership in the modern world of business, this chapter offers insights into the art of effective leadership in the 21st century.

6

"Global Entrepreneurship and the Future of Business"

In a world characterized by increasing globalization, entrepreneurship has evolved into a global phenomenon with significant implications for economies, societies, and the future of business. This chapter explores the global dimensions of entrepreneurship and the ways in which entrepreneurs are shaping the future of business on a worldwide scale.

6.1: The Global Entrepreneurship Landscape

We begin by examining the global entrepreneurship landscape, highlighting the diverse range of opportunities and challenges that entrepreneurs face in different regions and industries.

6.2: Cross-Border Ventures

Entrepreneurs are no longer confined by geographical borders. We explore how entrepreneurs are launching cross-border ventures and the unique challenges and opportunities they encounter in the global marketplace.

6.3: The Digital Revolution and Global Reach

The digital revolution has made it easier than ever for entrepreneurs to reach a global audience. We delve into the ways in which technology has transformed international business and allowed startups to scale quickly.

6.4: The Role of International Trade

Global entrepreneurs often engage in international trade. We discuss the importance of trade agreements, globalization, and the impact of trade policies on entrepreneurial ventures.

6.5: Social Entrepreneurship on a Global Scale

Social entrepreneurship is making a significant impact worldwide. We explore how entrepreneurs are addressing global challenges, from poverty to environmental sustainability, through innovative business models.

6.6: Cultural Sensitivity and Market Adaptation

Understanding and respecting diverse cultures is essential for global entrepreneurs. We discuss how entrepreneurs adapt their products and strategies to resonate with different markets.

6.7: The Challenges of Regulatory Compliance

Navigating complex international regulations can be a major challenge for global entrepreneurs. We explore the importance of compliance, legal frameworks, and the role of international organizations.

6.8: International Funding and Investment

Access to international funding and investment is critical for global entrepreneurs. We discuss how entrepreneurs secure international capital and the importance of understanding global investment trends.

6.9: Global Networks and Collaboration

Building global networks and fostering collaboration with international partners are crucial for success. We explore how entrepreneurs establish and leverage these connections.

6.10: Global Entrepreneurship Ecosystems

Different regions have developed their entrepreneurial ecosystems. We look at entrepreneurial hubs worldwide and the unique attributes that make them attractive to startups.

6.11: The Future of Global Entrepreneurship

We conclude by speculating on the future of global entrepreneurship, considering trends like remote work, the continued impact of technology, and the potential for global challenges to drive entrepreneurial innovation.

Throughout this chapter, readers will gain insights into the dynamic and interconnected world of global entrepreneurship. Whether you're an aspiring global entrepreneur, an investor interested in international markets, or simply someone curious about the future of business on a global scale, this chapter offers a comprehensive look at the exciting world of global entrepreneurship and its potential to shape the future of business.

7

"The Entrepreneurial Mindset: Skills and Strategies for Success"

Success in entrepreneurship often hinges on the mindset and skills of the individuals driving their ventures. In this chapter, we will delve into the entrepreneurial mindset, exploring the key attributes, strategies, and skills that entrepreneurs need to thrive in the 21st century.

7.1: The Growth Mindset

The growth mindset is a foundational concept in entrepreneurship. We'll explore how having a growth mindset, where challenges are seen as opportunities for learning and development, can propel entrepreneurs forward.

7.2: Resilience and Adaptability

Resilience is vital for entrepreneurs who must navigate uncertainty and setbacks. We'll discuss how to cultivate resilience and adaptability in the face of adversity.

7.3: Creative Problem-Solving

Creative problem-solving is at the heart of entrepreneurship. We'll examine how entrepreneurs approach challenges with innovative solutions and techniques to foster creative thinking.

7.4: Risk-Taking and Decision-Making

Entrepreneurs must make important decisions and take calculated risks. We'll discuss how to assess risks, make informed choices, and manage uncertainty effectively.

7.5: Time Management and Productivity

Effective time management and productivity are crucial for entrepreneurial success. We'll explore strategies and tools to help entrepreneurs stay organized and maximize their output.

7.6: Financial Literacy

Financial management is a key skill for entrepreneurs. We'll discuss the basics of financial literacy, budgeting, forecasting, and securing funding for ventures.

7.7: Marketing and Sales Skills

Marketing and sales are fundamental to business success. We'll examine the skills needed to create effective marketing strategies and close deals with customers.

7.8: Negotiation Skills

Negotiation is a core entrepreneurial skill. We'll explore the art of negotiation, from pricing and contracts to partnerships and collaborations.

7.9: Leadership and Team Building

Successful entrepreneurs often lead teams. We'll discuss how to build and lead a high-performing team, emphasizing communication, motivation, and conflict resolution.

7.10: Networking and Relationship Building

Effective networking and relationship building open doors for entrepreneurs. We'll explore strategies for connecting with mentors, customers, investors, and industry peers.

7.11: Effective Communication

Clear and persuasive communication is crucial in entrepreneurship. We'll discuss how entrepreneurs convey their ideas and vision to various stakeholders.

7.12: Strategic Planning and Goal Setting

Strategic planning and goal setting are essential for long-term success. We'll explore how entrepreneurs define goals and create roadmaps for their ventures.

By the end of this chapter, readers will have a comprehensive understanding of the mindset, skills, and strategies that underpin entrepreneurial success. Whether you're an aspiring entrepreneur looking to develop your skill set or someone interested in understanding the mindset of successful business leaders, this chapter offers valuable insights into the world of entrepreneurship in the 21st century.

8

"Ethics and Social Responsibility in Entrepreneurship"

In the 21st century, entrepreneurs are increasingly recognizing the significance of ethics and social responsibility in their ventures. This chapter explores the ethical considerations and social responsibilities that entrepreneurs face, as they strive to build successful businesses while making a positive impact on society.

8.1: The Intersection of Ethics and Entrepreneurship

We begin by examining the ethical dilemmas entrepreneurs encounter, including issues related to honesty, transparency, fair competition, and the treatment of employees, customers, and the environment.

8.2: Business Ethics and Decision-Making

We delve into the role of ethics in decision-making and how entrepreneurs can incorporate ethical considerations into their business strategies.

8.3: Ethical Leadership

Ethical leadership sets the tone for an organization's culture. We explore how ethical entrepreneurs lead by example, fostering integrity and moral values within their ventures.

8.4: Social Responsibility and Sustainability

Entrepreneurs are increasingly embracing social responsibility and sustainability in their business practices. We discuss how businesses can address environmental, social, and governance (ESG) issues.

8.5: Corporate Social Responsibility (CSR)

CSR has become a significant aspect of modern business. We explore how entrepreneurs are implementing CSR initiatives, from charitable contributions to sustainable business practices.

8.6: Impact Investing and Social Entrepreneurship

We discuss the emergence of impact investing and social entrepreneurship, where ventures are established with the primary goal of addressing social or environmental challenges.

8.7: Ethical Marketing and Customer Trust

Ethical marketing is essential for building trust with customers. We explore the principles of ethical marketing and how they impact brand reputation.

8.8: Fair Labor Practices

We examine the importance of fair labor practices and how entrepreneurs can ensure that their employees are treated with respect and fairness.

8.9: Environmental Stewardship

Entrepreneurs can play a critical role in environmental protection. We discuss sustainable practices, eco-friendly products, and the reduction of a business's carbon footprint.

8.10: Social Impact Measurement

Measuring the social impact of entrepreneurial ventures is a complex but essential task. We explore methods and metrics used to assess a business's positive contributions to society.

8.11: Ethical Challenges and Controversies

Ethical challenges can be complex, and entrepreneurs may face ethical controversies. We discuss real-world case studies and how entrepreneurs address these issues.

8.12: The Future of Ethical Entrepreneurship

We conclude by considering the future of ethical entrepreneurship, with a focus on the growing role of ethics and social responsibility in the business world.

By the end of this chapter, readers will have gained a deep understanding of the ethical considerations and social responsibilities that entrepreneurs face in the 21st century. Whether you are an aspiring entrepreneur or someone interested in the ethical dimensions of business, this chapter provides valuable insights into the evolving landscape of ethics and social responsibility in entrepreneurship.

9

"Innovation and the Impact of Technology on Entrepreneurship"

Technology has fundamentally transformed the entrepreneurial landscape in the 21st century, providing new tools, opportunities, and challenges for entrepreneurs. In this chapter, we explore the role of technology and innovation in shaping modern entrepreneurship and how entrepreneurs leverage these forces to drive their ventures forward.

9.1: The Digital Revolution and Entrepreneurship

We begin by examining how the digital revolution has reshaped the entrepreneurial landscape, enabling new business models, industries, and opportunities.

9.2: Technology as a Catalyst for Innovation

Technology acts as a catalyst for innovation. We discuss how entrepreneurs leverage emerging technologies to create groundbreaking solutions and drive their ventures forward.

9.3: The Rise of E-Commerce and Online Marketplaces

E-commerce and online marketplaces have revolutionized the way entrepreneurs do business. We explore the growth of online retail and the opportunities it presents.

9.4: Mobile Technology and Entrepreneurship

Mobile technology has become a cornerstone of modern entrepreneurship. We discuss how entrepreneurs develop mobile apps, services, and businesses that cater to the mobile-first world.

9.5: Big Data and Analytics

Big data and analytics have provided entrepreneurs with powerful insights. We explore how data-driven decision-making and analytics are transforming businesses.

9.6: Artificial Intelligence (AI) and Machine Learning

AI and machine learning are driving innovation across various industries. We delve into how entrepreneurs are harnessing these technologies for automation, personalization, and efficiency.

9.7: The Internet of Things (IoT) and Connectivity

IoT is expanding the possibilities for entrepreneurs. We discuss how IoT devices and connectivity are opening doors for new business opportunities.

9.8: Blockchain and Cryptocurrencies

Blockchain technology and cryptocurrencies are disrupting traditional finance and creating new avenues for entrepreneurs. We explore the potential and challenges of this space.

9.9: Augmented and Virtual Reality (AR/VR)

AR and VR technologies are reshaping industries like gaming, education, and healthcare. We discuss how entrepreneurs are embracing these immersive technologies.

9.10: Cybersecurity and Privacy

As technology advances, so do cybersecurity threats. We examine the importance of cybersecurity in modern business and the challenges entrepreneurs face in safeguarding data and customer privacy.

9.11: Tech Startups and Innovation Hubs

Tech startups and innovation hubs are at the forefront of technological innovation. We explore how these entrepreneurial ecosystems foster creativity and breakthroughs.

9.12: The Future of Technology and Entrepreneurship

We conclude by considering the future of technology and its potential to continue transforming entrepreneurship, from AI-driven ventures to space exploration and beyond.

10

"Challenges and Opportunities in 21st Century Entrepreneurship"

The world of entrepreneurship in the 21st century is rife with both challenges and opportunities. This chapter explores some of the most pressing issues and promising developments in the realm of entrepreneurship, shedding light on what aspiring entrepreneurs, business leaders, and stakeholders can expect as they navigate this dynamic landscape.

10.1: The Global Entrepreneurial Ecosystem

We begin by taking a comprehensive look at the global entrepreneurial ecosystem, examining how it has evolved, and the ways in which it continues to influence and shape the business world.

10.2: Economic and Market Challenges

Entrepreneurs face a range of economic and market challenges, from economic downturns and market volatility to competitive pressures. We discuss how entrepreneurs can adapt and thrive in such environments.

10.3: Technological Disruption

The rapid pace of technological advancement can disrupt established industries and business models. We explore the challenges and opportunities that entrepreneurs face as they navigate this landscape.

10.4: Access to Funding

Access to capital remains a significant challenge for many entrepreneurs. We delve into the various funding options, from venture capital to crowdfunding, and how to secure financial support for ventures.

10.5: Talent and Workforce Challenges

Entrepreneurs often encounter difficulties in recruiting and retaining top talent. We discuss strategies for building and maintaining high-performing teams.

10.6: Regulatory and Legal Hurdles

Navigating complex regulatory and legal landscapes can be a barrier to entrepreneurial success. We explore how entrepreneurs manage compliance and legal challenges.

10.7: Sustainability and Social Responsibility

The growing emphasis on sustainability and social responsibility presents opportunities for entrepreneurs. We discuss how businesses can align with these values while also achieving financial success.

10.8: Market Expansion and Globalization

Entrepreneurs often aspire to expand into global markets. We explore the challenges and strategies for international growth and market penetration.

10.9: The Gig Economy and Freelancing

The rise of the gig economy and freelancing presents both opportunities and challenges for entrepreneurs. We discuss how businesses can leverage these trends and address issues like workforce management and job security.

10.10: Education and Skill Development

Entrepreneurs need continuous learning and skill development. We explore the importance of ongoing education and how to stay ahead in the rapidly evolving business landscape.

10.11: Post-Pandemic Entrepreneurship

The COVID-19 pandemic has reshaped the entrepreneurial landscape. We discuss how entrepreneurs have adapted and the potential long-term impacts on the world of business.

10.12: The Future of Entrepreneurship

We conclude by considering the future of entrepreneurship, discussing emerging trends, areas of innovation, and the evolving role of entrepreneurship in shaping our world.

11

"The Entrepreneurial Journey: Stories from the Frontlines"

In this chapter, we will delve into the real-life stories of entrepreneurs who have embarked on their entrepreneurial journeys in the 21st century. Their experiences, trials, and triumphs will provide valuable insights for aspiring entrepreneurs, as they navigate the complexities and uncertainties of building and growing their businesses.

11.1: The Start-Up Phase

We begin by exploring the early stages of entrepreneurship, as entrepreneurs take their initial ideas and turn them into viable businesses. We'll share the stories of entrepreneurs who faced the challenges of market research, business planning, and securing initial funding.

11.2: Navigating Challenges and Adversities

Entrepreneurship is not without its challenges. We'll delve into the stories of entrepreneurs who encountered setbacks, such as financial struggles, product failures, and market downturns, and how they persevered.

11.3: Growth and Scaling

As businesses grow, entrepreneurs face new challenges and opportunities. We'll explore stories of entrepreneurs who successfully scaled their businesses, including the strategies they employed and the lessons they learned.

11.4: Innovation and Disruption

Innovation is at the core of entrepreneurship. We'll share stories of entrepreneurs who disrupted industries and created groundbreaking products or services, offering insights into their creative processes.

11.5: Social Impact and Ethical Entrepreneurship

Many entrepreneurs prioritize social impact and ethical business practices. We'll feature stories of entrepreneurs who have integrated social responsibility into their ventures, making a positive difference in society.

11.6: Global Entrepreneurship

Globalization has opened doors for entrepreneurs to expand internationally. We'll discuss the journeys of entrepreneurs who have taken their businesses global and the challenges they encountered along the way.

11.7: Lessons from Failure

Not all entrepreneurial journeys lead to success. We'll share stories of entrepreneurs who faced failure and the valuable lessons they gained from these experiences.

11.8: Technology and Digital Transformation

The impact of technology is evident in many entrepreneurial journeys. We'll explore stories of tech entrepreneurs who harnessed digital innovation to disrupt traditional industries.

11.9: Sustainability and Green Entrepreneurship

Sustainability is an essential consideration for modern entrepreneurs. We'll highlight stories of entrepreneurs who have built businesses with a focus on environmental and social responsibility.

11.10: The Future of Entrepreneurship

We conclude the chapter by considering the future of entrepreneurship. We'll explore the stories of forward-thinking entrepreneurs who are shaping the next era of business and innovation.

12

"Entrepreneurship and the Evolving Business Landscape"

In this final chapter, we will explore how entrepreneurship continues to evolve and adapt to the changing business landscape of the 21st century. We will examine emerging trends, challenges, and opportunities that entrepreneurs and business leaders face as they navigate the ever-shifting terrain of modern business.

12.1: The Post-Pandemic Business World

The COVID-19 pandemic has left a lasting impact on the business world. We'll discuss how entrepreneurs are adapting to the post-pandemic landscape, including the rise of remote work, digital transformation, and the resilience of various industries.

12.2: Sustainability and Eco-Friendly Entrepreneurship

Sustainability has become a driving force in modern business. We'll explore how entrepreneurs are incorporating eco-friendly practices and products into their ventures to meet consumer demands and address environmental challenges.

12.3: The Role of Artificial Intelligence and Automation

Artificial intelligence and automation are transforming various industries. We'll discuss the opportunities and challenges presented by these technologies and how entrepreneurs are leveraging them for efficiency and innovation.

12.4: The Gig Economy and Flexible Work Arrangements

The gig economy is on the rise, offering flexible work arrangements. We'll explore how this trend is shaping entrepreneurship, from the rise of freelancers and independent contractors to changes in workforce dynamics.

12.5: New Funding Models and Investment Trends

Entrepreneurs have access to diverse funding models and investment trends. We'll discuss the emergence of alternative financing methods, including crowdfunding, impact investing, and special purpose acquisition companies (SPACs).

12.6: Diversity, Equity, and Inclusion in Business

The importance of diversity, equity, and inclusion (DEI) is gaining prominence in entrepreneurship. We'll explore how businesses are promoting DEI in their workforce and decision-making processes.

12.7: The Evolving Regulatory Landscape

Regulations and compliance standards are continuously evolving. We'll discuss how entrepreneurs are navigating complex legal and regulatory challenges, from data privacy to industry-specific regulations.

12.8: The Future of Work and Workplace Culture

The concept of work and workplace culture is evolving. We'll examine the impact of remote work, hybrid work models, and the changing expectations of the workforce.

12.9: Emerging Business Models

New and innovative business models are emerging. We'll explore how entrepreneurs are redefining traditional business models to better serve their customers and adapt to changing market dynamics.

12.10: Entrepreneurship in Emerging Markets

Entrepreneurship is not limited to established economies. We'll discuss how entrepreneurs in emerging markets are driving economic growth and innovation, even with unique challenges.

12.11: The Future of Entrepreneurship

We conclude by considering the future of entrepreneurship. We'll explore what's on the horizon, from space exploration and biotechnology to the potential for breakthrough innovations that will shape the next era of business and entrepreneurship.

"Success Stories of 21st Century Entrepreneurs" is a comprehensive book with twelve chapters that delve into the world of entrepreneurship in the 21st century. Here's a summary of each chapter:

Chapter 1: "Success Stories of 21st Century Entrepreneurs"
  - This chapter introduces the book and highlights the remarkable success stories of entrepreneurs who have made a significant impact in the 21st

century.

Chapter 2: "Navigating the Entrepreneurial Landscape"
- Explores the fundamental principles and strategies for aspiring entrepreneurs to navigate the complex entrepreneurial landscape, including identifying opportunities, creating a business plan, building a team, securing funding, managing risks, marketing and branding, adapting to change, ethical considerations, and the role of technology and innovation.

Chapter 3: "Innovation and Disruption: The Engine of Entrepreneurship"
- Focuses on the critical role of innovation in entrepreneurship, covering the innovation mindset, creativity, market disruption, technology's role, research and development, open innovation, intellectual property, sustainability, innovation across industries, and the startup ecosystem.

Chapter 4: "The Entrepreneurial Ecosystem: Nurturing Success"
- Explores the various components of the entrepreneurial ecosystem, including government support, educational institutions, incubators and accelerators, investment, networking, access to resources, diversity and inclusion, measuring success, global perspectives, and the challenges and future of entrepreneurial ecosystems.

Chapter 5: "The Art of Leadership in Entrepreneurship"
- Examines the importance of leadership in entrepreneurship, covering aspects like the entrepreneurial leader's profile, leading by example, visionary leadership, team building, leading through change, decision-making, ethical leadership, resilience and adaptability, leadership styles, mentoring, and the legacy of entrepreneurial leadership.

Chapter 6: "Global Entrepreneurship and the Future of Business"
- Explores the global dimensions of entrepreneurship, including cross-border ventures, the impact of the digital revolution, international trade, social entrepreneurship, cultural sensitivity, and the challenges and opportu-

nities of global entrepreneurship.

Chapter 7: "The Entrepreneurial Mindset: Skills and Strategies for Success"
- Focuses on the entrepreneurial mindset, including the growth mindset, resilience, creative problem-solving, risk-taking, time management, financial literacy, marketing and sales skills, negotiation skills, leadership, networking, effective communication, and strategic planning.

Chapter 8: "Ethics and Social Responsibility in Entrepreneurship"
- Explores the ethical considerations and social responsibilities entrepreneurs face, covering business ethics, decision-making, ethical leadership, social responsibility, corporate social responsibility, impact investing, ethical marketing, fair labor practices, environmental stewardship, social impact measurement, ethical challenges, and the future of ethical entrepreneurship.

Chapter 9: "Innovation and the Impact of Technology on Entrepreneurship"
- Examines the role of technology and innovation in modern entrepreneurship, including the digital revolution, technology as a catalyst for innovation, e-commerce, mobile technology, big data, AI and machine learning, IoT, blockchain, AR/VR, cybersecurity, and tech startups.

Chapter 10: "Challenges and Opportunities in 21st Century Entrepreneurship"
- Explores the challenges and opportunities entrepreneurs face in the modern business landscape, including the global entrepreneurial ecosystem, economic and market challenges, technological disruption, access to funding, talent and workforce challenges, regulatory and legal hurdles, sustainability, market expansion, the gig economy, education and skill development, post-pandemic entrepreneurship, and the future of entrepreneurship.

Chapter 11: "The Entrepreneurial Journey: Stories from the Frontlines"
- Shares real-life stories of entrepreneurs at various stages of their journeys,

from startups to scaling, facing challenges, and making a positive social impact.

Chapter 12: "Entrepreneurship and the Evolving Business Landscape"
- Discusses the evolving business landscape, including the post-pandemic world, sustainability, AI and automation, the gig economy, funding models, DEI, regulatory changes, the future of work, emerging business models, entrepreneurship in emerging markets, and the future of entrepreneurship.

This book offers a comprehensive exploration of entrepreneurship in the 21st century, covering a wide range of topics and providing valuable insights for aspiring entrepreneurs and anyone interested in the dynamic world of business and innovation.